Tuning

When you tune, you correct the pitch of each string. Pitch refers to how high or low a musical tone is. This is adjusted by tightening (or loosening) the string, using the tuning pegs or fine tuners. The tighter the string, the higher the pitch.

Your violin strings should be tuned to the following pitches, from lowest to highest: G-D-A-E. When tightening the pegs, detune the instrument slightly, then tighten the string to the proper pitch. (You can detune the violin by loosening the strings a little bit.) Sometimes the pegs move quickly and in large turns, so be careful: a little too far and you might snap the string.

Orchestras generally use the note A-440 as their starting pitch. You can acquire this pitch several ways: a tuner; the A above middle C on the piano; an electronic metronome; or an electronic tuner. If you have a mobile device (smart phone, tablet, iPad), I recommend purchasing the ClearTune app. (Many free tuner apps are not very good.)

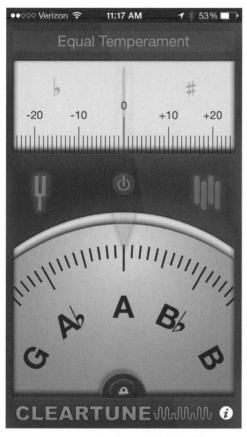

ClearTune app

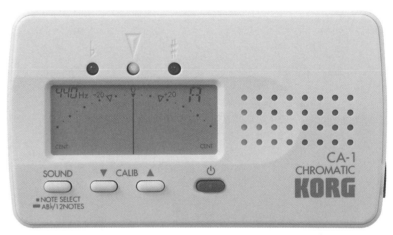

Korg CA-1 Chromatic Tuner

Other Tuning Methods

If you don't own a mobile device or a tuner, use an electronic piano to get the A — and the other pitches as well. See the picture below. Middle C is given as a reference; it does not correspond to the pitch of a violin string.

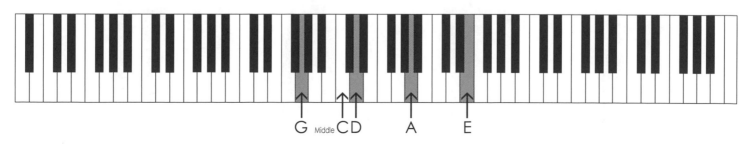

G   Middle C D   A   E

A FEW MORE THINGS

Sitting versus Standing Posture

There's no doubt about it, playing standing up is the most comfortable way to play violin. However, we find ourselves sitting in orchestras, chamber groups, or extended practice sessions. It's crucial that you sit and stand correctly.

Below are step-by-step picture instructions on how to prepare yourself to stand properly and how to hold the instrument properly in playing position. Once that is set, follow the step-by-step picture diagram on how to hold your bow. You might want to visit LearnFiddle. com to download the free videos that walk you through this process as well.

Correct standing posture.   Rest position.   Step 1:
Notice the feet.   Step 2:
Again, notice the feet.   Step 3.

Step 4:
Come from above.   Step 5.   Step 6: Bow comes to the strings from above.   Step 7: Bow is now on the strings.

Violin 1

INTRODUCTION

You bought a violin... so now what?

Congratulations! You look great holding that new violin (even standing in front of the mirror imagining yourself on a concert stage or fiddling at the Grand Ole Opry). But won't your friends and family be even more impressed if you can actually play the darn thing? In just a few weeks, you'll be playing some well-known tunes and jamming on some new ones.

All we ask is that you observe the three **P**s: **P**atience, **P**ractice and **P**ace yourself.

Don't try to bite off more than you can chew, and DON'T skip ahead. If your hands hurt or your neck feels stiff, take the day off. If you get frustrated, put it down and come back later. If you forget something, go back and learn it again. If you're having a great time, forget about dinner and keep on playing. Most importantly, have fun!

ABOUT THE AUDIO

Glad you noticed the added bonus – audio tracks! All the music examples in this book are included with the audio, so you can hear how they sound first and play along when you're ready. Take a listen whenever you see this symbol: ◆1

Each audio example is preceded by count-off "clicks" to help you feel the beat before the music starts. If the tempo (speed) is too fast for you, no problem! The audio is also enhanced with **Playback+**, a multi-functional audio that allows you to adjust the recording to any tempo without changing the pitch, set loop points, change keys, pan left or right – available exclusively from Hal Leonard!

To access audio visit:
www.halleonard.com/mylibrary
Enter Code
4854-5735-4003-4631

ISBN 978-1-4950-0930-3

HAL•LEONARD®
CORPORATION
7777 W. BLUEMOUND RD. P.O. BOX 13819 MILWAUKEE, WI 53213

In Australia Contact:
Hal Leonard Australia Pty. Ltd.
4 Lentara Court
Cheltenham, Victoria, 3192 Australia
Email: ausadmin@halleonard.com.au

Visit Hal Leonard Online at
www.halleonard.com

A GOOD PLACE TO START

To understand the instruction in this book, you need to know the parts of your instrument. The pictures below will help. Take time to get acquainted with the parts of your violin and bow.

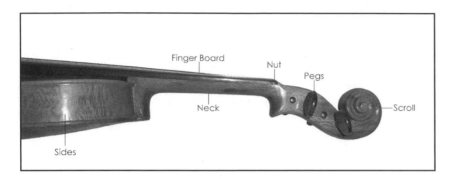

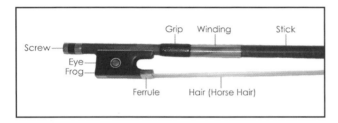

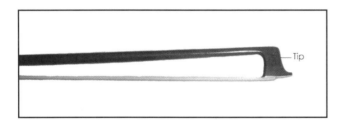

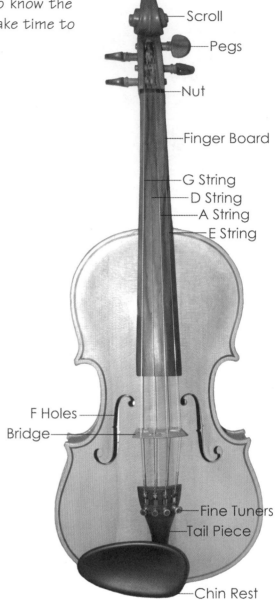

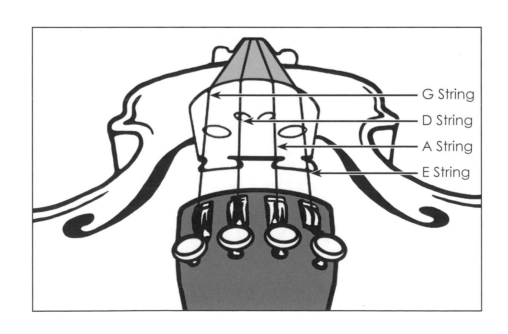

Ring finger and middle finger are "buddies."

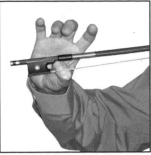

Thumb is bent and touches the bow hair.

Middle finger and ring finger are still "buddies."

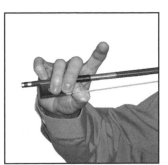

The pinkie finger is bent, and the tip of the finger touches the bow.

The stick of the bow sits between the first and second knuckle of the index finger.

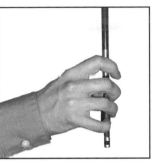

Additional view of the proper bow hold.

Additional view of the proper bow hold.

Picture This

Below is a picture of finger-tape placements and an illustration of the left hand. The fingers will land directly on the finger tapes. You may want to take your instrument to a violin teacher or music store to have them help you put on finger tapes. It's important that they be placed correctly.

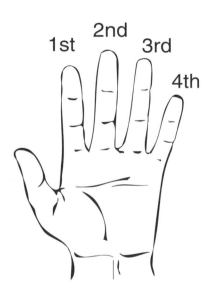

Left-hand fingers are numbered 1 through 4. (Pianists: Note that the thumb is not number 1)

DOG-EAR THESE TWO PAGES
(...you'll need to review them later)

Music is a language with its own symbols, structure, and rules (and exceptions to those rules). Reading, writing, and playing music requires that you know the symbols and rules. But let's take it one step at a time (a few now, a few later)...

Notes

Music is written with little doo-hickeys called **notes**. They come in many shapes and sizes, but each one has two main characteristics: its **pitch** (indicated by its position on the staff) and its **rhythmic value** (indicated by the following symbols):

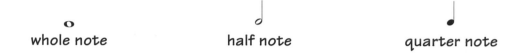

The rhythmic value tells you how many beats the note lasts. Most commonly, a quarter note equals one beat. After that, it's just like fractions. (Yeah, we hate math, too!)

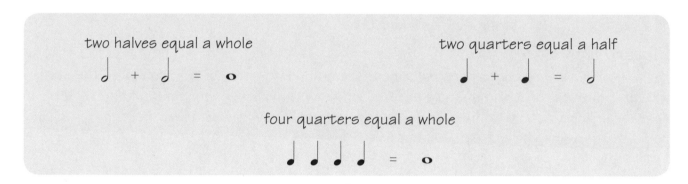

Staff

Notes are positioned on (or near) a **staff**, which consists of five parallel lines and four spaces. (The plural for staff is "staves.") Each line and space represents a different pitch.

Ledger Lines

Since all notes won't fit on just five lines and four spaces, short **ledger lines** are used to temporarily extend the staff:

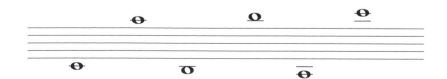

Clef

A funky symbol called a **clef** indicates which pitches are represented on the staff. Music uses a variety of clefs for different instruments, but you only need to learn about one—the **treble clef**.

Treble clef

A treble clef makes the lines and spaces on the staff have the following pitches:

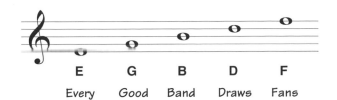

E	G	B	D	F
Every	Good	Band	Draws	Fans

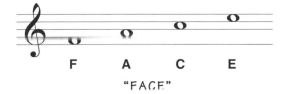

F	A	C	E
		"FACE"	

An easy way to remember the line pitches (from bottom to top) is "Every **G**ood **B**and **D**raws **F**ans." The spaces simply spell the word "**FACE**."

Measures (or Bars)

Notes on a staff are divided into **measures** (or "bars") to help you keep track of where you are in the song. (Imagine reading a book without any periods, commas, or capital letters!)

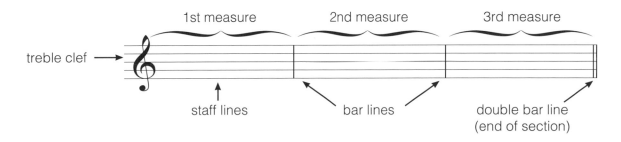

Time Signatures (or Meters)

A **time signature** (or "meter") indicates how the beats in each measure will be counted. It contains two numbers: the top number tells you how many beats will be in each measure, and the bottom number tells you which type of note will equal one beat.

four beats per measure
quarter note (1/4) = one beat

three beats per measure
quarter note (1/4) = one beat

☞   **R**elax for a while, read through all this again later, and then move on.
(Trust us—as you go through the book, you'll start to understand this stuff.)

LESSON 1

Don't just stand there. Play something!

We've tuned. We're relaxed. We're comfortable. And we're eager to play. Let's get down to business.

As you prepare to play, you need to remember a few things.
1. Keep your bow moving. Your bow strokes for these next few lessons should be about 4-6 inches long each time.
2. Make sure you're in the middle of the bow.
3. Keep your bow equally between the bridge and the finger board at all times.
4. Try to keep your bow hair flat.
5. Avoid squeezing in either hand.

Bowing on Open Strings

Many teachers and players alike agree: There is an art to using the bow; it is the most difficult part of playing violin. So, we're going to take the left hand completely out of the equation for our intial exercise. Let's do this on the A string first, with no fingers. Keep in mind the position of your elbow here. Make sure the elevation is correct. Refer to the picture on page 9 that illustrates the proper placement of your bow-arm elbow.

Set your metronome to 60bpm. This will be the quarter-note (♩) pulse. Pull the bow every time you hear the click of the metronome. You'll notice two quarter rests in between each set of quarter notes. Those too will line up with each click of the metronome. While you are "resting" between notes, say "re-set" aloud. While you speak the syllables, re-set your bow to be in the proper position and placement.

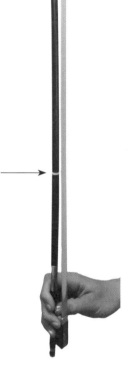

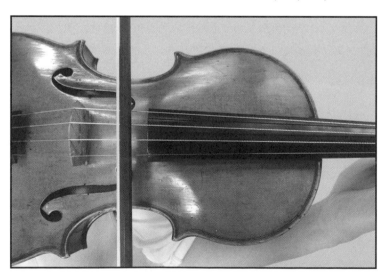

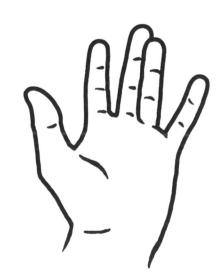

The illustration at the right shows the finger pattern you should be using when you first start out. Notice the middle and ring finger touching. This is important to note as you move into placing your fingers. That feeling should be something you use to help you know you're doing it right.

Your left hand will look like this.

Play the A string open, with no fingers down. The note is indicated on a treble staff:

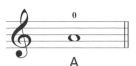

Your right arm will look like this.

Your left arm will look like this.

You will see some markings above the first note in each measure that look like this: ⊓. This is called a down-bow. The down-bow is a motion that moves away from your body in a downward motion. In contrast, the up-bow looks like this: V. The movement for the up-bow is the opposite of the down-bow.

Now, let's add the fingers. Make certain your left hand is placed properly and your wrist is in a neutral position. Be sure your elbow is in an A-string position. The A-string elbow position allows your bow to move up and down on the A string, while maintaining a proper bow hold, proper pressure and bow weight on the string, and keeps you on the A string only. Refer to the picture above for proper elbow placement.

Continuing, place your first finger (index finger) on the first finger tape, sounding the note B. The remaining fingers should hover over the A string. The same principles apply as you put the subsequent fingers down.

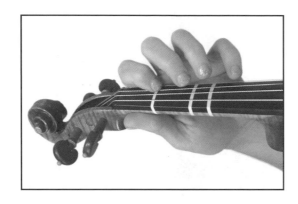

Play the A string with your first finger down. This note lies on the middle line of the treble clef staff:

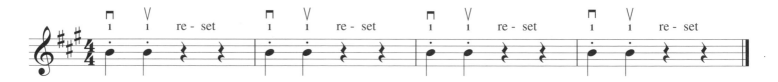

To play the note C♯, we add the second finger.

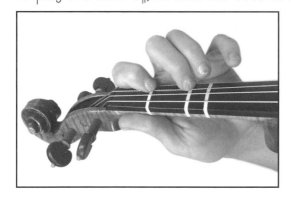

Play the A string with your second finger down and you get C♯, which lies on the space just above B:

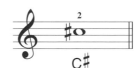

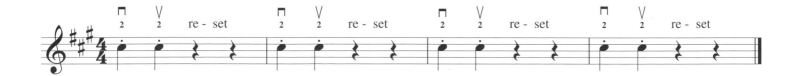

Add the third finger to play the note D.

Play the A string with your third finger down and you have D. It sits just above C#:

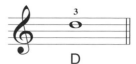

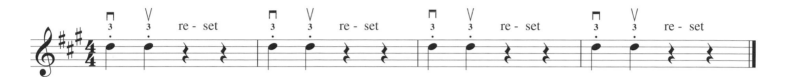

In the following tune, we add each finger in order, both up and down the neck. Remember, for now, to keep your fingers down as you add them.

◆1 A–B–C–D

Each audio example is preceded by count-off "clicks" to help you feel the beat before the music starts. You can pan right to hear only the metronome – or pan left to hear only the violin demo. **Using Playback +,** you can also adjust the tempo.

Here's a good exercise for placing the fingers. In the example below, take one bar to walk your fingers up without using the bow. Play from there. In measure 10, walk your fingers up silently again, then play in measure 11.

◆ Silent Fingers Song

☞ **Repeat signs** (|: :|) tell you to (you guessed it!) repeat everything in between. If only one sign appears (:|), repeat from the beginning of the piece.

You now have four notes under your fingers, so let's play a real song. Walk those fingers silently up to C♯ and start from there.

◆ Boil Them Cabbage Down
A Major Version

LESSON 2
Moving on...

Welcome back! Now you know four notes and a song. Okay, so they might have been a bit boring, but nonetheless important to build your technique and make playing further songs easier.

HELPFUL HINT: Whenever you start practicing, make sure your violin is in tune. Flip back to page 3 and double check. (If the dog starts howling, it probably isn't.)

The D String

We can apply what we've learned on the A string to the D string, playing some of the tunes we learned for the A string with the D string. We'll use the same finger pattern. The only difference is the right-elbow elevation, which is slightly higher; also, the left-elbow placement is moved in, or forward, from the A-string position.

Play the D string open, with no fingers down. The note D is indicated on a treble clef staff like this:

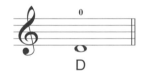

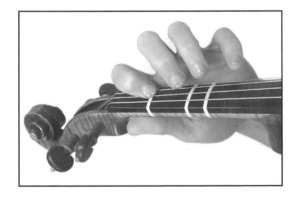

Play the D string with first finger down. The note E is indicated on a treble clef staff like this:

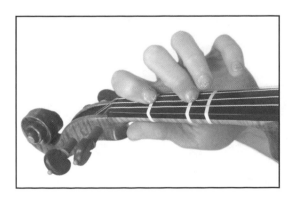

Play the D string with second finger down. The note F♯ is indicated on a treble clef staff like this:

Play the D string with third finger down. The note G is indicated on a treble clef staff like this:

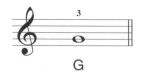

G

Your left elbow will look like this.

Your right elbow will look like this.

Practice your new notes with this short exercise.

◆ D–E–F–G

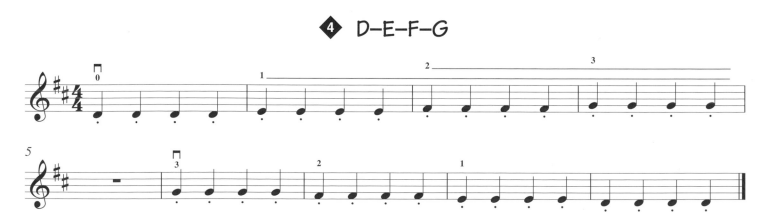

You want to get comfortable with this string, so continue with a tune that should sound familiar.

⑤ Boil Them Cabbage Down
D Major Version

Fingering Tip: When playing this next piece, make sure all the fingers behind the one you're putting down are being set and lifted at exactly the same time. This provides the support for you to play the note clearly. If your rhythm isn't precise, you will have extra notes played along with the note you intend to play. Take it slow and relax.

⑥ Sweet Summer Time

YOU GOT RHYTHM

Can you spare a quarter? How about an eighth?

An **eighth note** has a flag on it: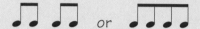

Two eighth notes equal one quarter note (or one beat in 4/4 and 3/4). To make it easier on the eyes, eighth notes are connected with a beam, like this:

To count eighth notes, divide the beat in half and say "and" between the beats:

Practice this by first counting out loud while tapping your foot on the beat.
Then play the notes while counting and tapping. How's that for multi-tasking?

What about the eighth rest?

Good question – glad you're paying attention! An eighth rest looks like this: ⅞
Eighth rests are just like eighth notes, but you... pause instead of playing a note.
Count, tap, play, and pause with the following example:

Crossing Strings

Although we've already done a small bit of string crossing, the next string crossing involves preparing one elbow earlier than the other. This will take some getting used to. Remember, whichever hand is playing on a particular string, allow your elbow to be in a position that lets your arms and fingers move freely. "Rock" your elbows to the appropriate string position respective to each arm. In your left hand, make sure your fingers always hover over the string they are about to play – or are currently playing – and that your wrist is straight and relaxed.

For this variation on "Twinkle, Twinkle Little Star," prepare your third finger, the note G, before you try to play the entire line. Getting ready in a relaxed way will ensure that you don't panic when you actually put it down. It's like calling in for takeout and it's just been boxed up when you arrive. Nice and easy – in theory, at least.

7 Twinkle, Twinkle Little Star
Cha Cha Version 1

The following variation on "Twinkle, Twinkle Little Star" is a little harder, because you have to make the transitions from one note to the next a little faster. This etude might take some time. Be patient and relax and you'll have it perfected in short order.

⑧ Twinkle, Twinkle Little Star

Another Variation

The Legato Stroke

The legato stroke is difficult to master because it forces you to increase the flexibility of your wrist. Ideally, it is a smooth, connected stroke that uses the entire bow, tip to frog. We are going to use the same finger pattern from the previous two pieces and apply it to this new bowing style. The idea is to keep the bow moving, almost without stopping. See if you can (almost) hide the change of direction at either end of the bow.

⑨ Twinkle, Twinkle Little Star

Theme

LESSON 3

Three's company...

Wow – you've learned so much already! At this rate, you'll be ready for a recording contract next week. (Okay, maybe not.) Are you ready to learn a new string? Make sure you're in tune and let's get to work.

The G String

The G string is the thickest and lowest string on the violin. Make sure your left elbow is rocked nicely in and that your knuckle is elevated to the appropriate height. Your right elbow will also be elevated – to allow you to get over to this string. You may want to pace yourself here. Keeping your arm elevated this high for long periods of time can be strenuous at first.

Play the G string open, with no fingers down. The low G note is indicated on a treble clef staff like this:

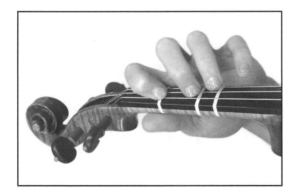

Play the G string with first finger down. The low A note is indicated on a treble clef staff like this:

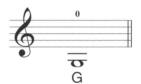

Play the G string with second finger down. The low B note is indicated on a treble clef staff like this:

Play the G string with third finger down. Middle C is indicated on a treble clef staff like this:

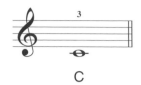

C

Your left elbow will look like this.

Your right elbow will look like this.

Practice walking your fingers up in the normal finger pattern, playing the cha-cha rhythm used for the Twinkle Variation.

🔟 Cha Cha Walking Fingers

Moving forward, practice this slightly easier piece. It is designed to get you ready for some jumping around we're about to do.

⓫ A Stroll in the Park

Try this short exercise. Remember, you're going to be skipping fingers now. Try to pace yourself and relax as you put your fingers down. This will take some practice, but it will really help your playing.

⓬ Hop, Skip & Jump

Now that we are adding a low 2, we should discuss the difference between the note names. High 2, as many call it, is what you've already played in the beginning. If you look at the key signatures of all of your previous pieces, this information is communicated to you by putting a sharp sign (♯) on the space that denotes C. The key signature is just a collection of sharps or flats (or even a lack thereof) at the beginning of every line of music. In your case, we've used only sharps in the key signature. The sharp sign raises the pitch a half step from where it normally occurs, creating a C♯. We put it in the key signature so that we don't have to write the sharp sign next to every occurrence of the note C♯. By keeping it in the key signature, we know that, unless there is something that tells us otherwise, we always play high 2. It keeps the piece looking clean and makes it easier to read.

Now that we are working with low 2, we are lowering the C♯ down to its "natural" position. This can be done two ways. We can keep the C♯ in the key signature and write a natural sign (♮) next to every note to tell us to play the C in its natural position every time, or we could do what we've done instead. We decided to leave out the sharp sign in the key signature, again to keep things clean. When you don't see the sharp sign next to the note or in the key signature, we know it will be played as a low 2, or C♮, respectively. (You will never see a natural sign in a key signature.) So, it's just implied that if there is no sharp on the line or space, the note is being played in its natural position.

All this information may be confusing, so take a minute to let it sink in. After you have done that, remember that as you move forward in the book, you will need to pay attention to what sharps or flats (♭) may be in the key signature so that you know where exactly your finger has to go. Flats do the opposite of what the sharp sign does; they take the note from its "natural" state and lower it a half step. (Don't concern yourself with flats right now. We won't be using them much in this book, so let's stay focused on the sharps.)

There's still more to learn about the "low 2" – the low second finger. Previously, your finger pattern involved the second and third finger touching. We are going to alter that and move your second finger close to your first. You won't have a finger tape for this one, so listen closely to make sure it's in tune.

The finger pattern on the D and A strings now requires your first and second fingers to touch; your second and third fingers will touch on the G string. Remember this as you move forward and you should do well.

Play the A string with a low second finger down. The note C is indicated on a treble clef staff like this:

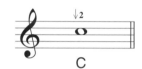

Play the D string with low second finger down. The note F is indicated on a treble clef staff like this:

◆13 Aura Lee

Let's get a little more practice with this low second finger concept! What follows is a simple version of a square dance tune that will give you a nice little workout.

◆14 Golden Slippers

LESSON 4
Climbing higher...

The E string is the highest string on the violin. Because of its high pitch, it can be the most unforgiving string on the instrument, so be careful and avoid squeezing and pushing. Use plenty of bow and trust your hands. You've been playing some rather advanced music already. Just move your elbows to the E string position and rock out.

Play the E string open, with no fingers down. The note is indicated on a treble clef staff like this:

Play the E string with first finger down. The note is indicated on a treble clef staff like this:

Play the E string with second finger down. The note is indicated on a treble clef staff like this:

Play the E string with third finger down. The note is indicated on a treble clef staff like this:

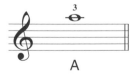

Your left elbow will look like this.

Your right elbow will look like this.

◆15 Twinkle, Twinkle Little Star
Cha Cha Variation 2

16 Walk and Skip

17 This Old Man

Review

We're more than halfway through the book, so now is an appropriate time to take a backward glance at what we've covered thus far. It's always a good idea to go back and play songs and etudes you've worked on previously, to keep those skills active and to help you move ahead. Let's review.

1. We began by getting acquainted with the parts of the violin and bow.

2. We discussed the importance of accurate tuning and looked at several tools to help achieve it.

3. Step-by-step instructions taught us how to sit properly, stand properly, and how to hold the violin and bow in playing position.

4. We learned several notes on the A string and the D string and looked at proper placement of both elbows.

5. Finger patterns provided a challenge. We worked these on several strings.

6. Eighth-note rhythms were introduced in the "cha cha" version of "Twinkle, Twinkle Little Star."

7. We added yet another finger pattern on focused on the "low 2" concept.

If you feel unsure about any of these concepts, take some time now to work through them once more. When you're ready, let's move ahead!

LESSON 5
Fancy fingerwork...

Your storehouse of violin knowledge is growing ever fuller. Let's increase the bounty by adding a couple of new fingers, a pickup measure, and a new time signature. (We'll cover those last two items in a moment.) The exercises that follow require us to use the fourth finger. We haven't done this before. Take a look at the picture below that shows the placement of the fourth finger. You will also notice that the fourth finger shares the same space as your open A string. That's because they are the same note! How about the fourth finger on the G string? That's shares the same space as open D. Again, same note!

The fourth finger is used in first position for many reasons, but the most common are to maximize efficiency by avoiding unneeded string crossings, and to add color and/or vibrato to that note. Vibrato is a technique we use to make the sound shake (vibrate) a bit. It adds warmth and beauty to the tone. You won't do this for a while, but being able to play the fourth finger in tune is a must.

"My First Waltz" (see page 30) is the longest and hardest piece you've played so far. Here's what you'll need to know to play it. First, you'll be using your fourth finger for the first time, so let's play a few exercises that will get you used to that.

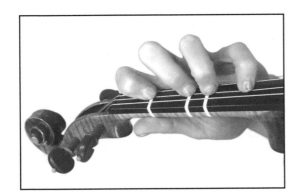

Play the D string with fourth finger down. The note is indicated on a treble clef staff like this:

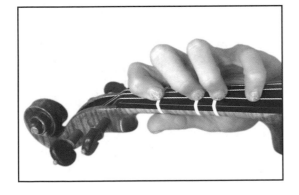

Play the G string with fourth finger down. The note is indicated on a treble clef staff like this:

18 D String Walk to 4

19 G String Walk to 4

Up next: the high third finger. Some work is required here, so you can try the next two exercises without the fourth finger. Then, once you feel comfortable, add the fourth finger. This will help you play "My First Waltz."

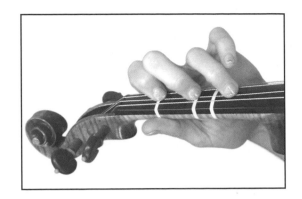

Play the D string with high third finger down. The note is indicated on a treble clef staff like this:

The new finger pattern, or high 3 finger pattern looks like this. Play the G string with high third finger down. The note is indicated on a treble clef staff like this:

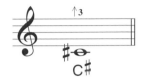

Note: In several of the tunes that follow, several "unnecessary" sharps have been added to the music notation — as a gentle reminder to keep a well-tuned high finger position.

20 D String Walk to 4 with High 3

21 G String Walk to 4 with High 3

Before you play your waltz, let's talk about the time signature and pickup measures. All the time signatures in this book so far have been in duple meter. Basically, everything fits together in a two- or four-beat measure. The time signature for "My First Waltz" is a triple meter. This means you'll counting to 3, then start over at 1 again. 3/4 is always the time signature for waltzes. Remember, when you play a waltz, an emphasis on beat 1 is customary. You'll have a feel of "strong-weak-weak" as you play.

"My First Waltz" also features a pickup measure. Pickup measures are partial measures employed to give a certain emphasis to a beat. Usually, that's beat 1. Working with pickup measures in waltzes helps the feel keep moving forward. So, why don't we try it out?

Pickups aren't just trucks...

Instead of starting a song with rests, a **pickup measure** can be used. A pickup measure simply deletes the rests. So, if a pickup has only one beat, you count "1, 2, 3" and start playing on beat 4:

22 My First Waltz
Version 1

LESSON 6
Ties, slurs, & dotted rhythms...

A tie and a slur look almost alike, but serve different purposes. Let's look at a slur first.

A **slur** is the connecting of two or more consecutive notes that creates the sound of a smooth transition between each note without changing the direction of your bow. See below.

separate notes   slurred notes

A **tie** is somewhat similar to a dotted rhythm. Both serve the same purpose: to lengthen a note's duration. Ties often are used between bar lines, while the dotted rhythm remains within the bar lines to keep the correct number of beats per measure. However, ties can also be used within bar lines.

YOU STILL GOT RHYTHM!

Nice tie!

A **tie** connects two notes and tells you to extend the first note to the end of the tied note:

1   2   3   (4   1)   (2)   3   (4   1   2)   3   4

Simple Simon! Remember to always count out loud until you begin to think and feel the beat.

The ones with dots are nice, too!

Another way to extend the value of a note is to use a **dot**. A dot extends the note by one-half of its value. Most common is the **dotted half** note:

$$\textrm{half note} \; + \; \textrm{dot} \; = \; \textrm{dotted half note}$$

half note   +   dot   =   dotted half note
(two beats)   (one beat)   (three beats)

You'll encounter dotted half notes in many songs, especially those that use 3/4 meter.

Use "My First Waltz" to practice the slur concept. You already know the notes, so just change the bowing according to how the slurs are indicated.

23 My First Waltz
Version 2

Next up: ties and dotted rhythms. Let's tackle the ties first. Remember to count in your mind. This can be tricky.

24 Like My Tie?

The next exercise looks different, but sounds exactly the same as the previous one. Notice how dots have replaced ties and notes.

25 Walking Over the Hilltop

LESSON 7

Since you were able to do that so well, let's revisit the low second finger idea. You've already played the low 2 on D and A, so let's go ahead and use the same technique on the E string. If you wish to employ the "Walk to 4" exercises on the D, A, and E strings first, go ahead! It's the same finger pattern on a different string, and worth trying before doing what's coming next.

Play the E string with low second finger down. The note is indicated on a treble clef staff like this:

Just a quick note about the patterns you've been playing so far. All the patterns have a pleasing "major" sound. These next two exercises will have a sadder "minor" sound. As you play, listen closely to see if you can hear the difference. It all has to do with the difference between your "regular" or "high" second finger and your "low" second finger.

26 A String Walk to 4 with Low 2

㉗ E String Walk to 4 with Low 2

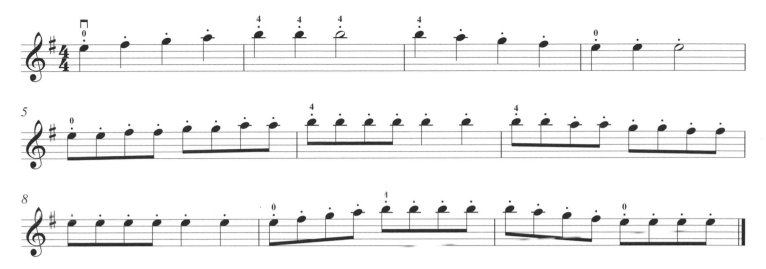

A Note About Accidentals

So far, we've used several different key signatures while teaching you the violin. This way, it has been easier for you not to have to learn too much note reading at one time. The sharp sign has been employed as an "accidental" to remind you to extend a finger. We did this when we were using high 3. In other words, the key signature already told us the third finger was supposed to be high. But as a "courtesy" you were reminded — just in case you might forget.

Now, we are using the accidental in a different way. In measure 9 of the next piece, you will notice a C♯. But if you look at the key signature, there is no C♯ there. This means that the composer, who happens to be me, intentionally changed this note for a reason. So, if you're not paying attention, you may "accidentally" miss it. (Pardon the pun.) This is the primary way we use accidentals; that's the big takeaway here.

Another important thing to remember about "true" accidentals, like the one you see in measure 9, is that the note stays changed until the end of the bar line. Then, unless it's raised again in the next measure, you will not play the note raised anymore. It reverts to whatever the key signature calls for.

If this confuses you, take a moment to read it again. It's a weird idea to get your head around.

Are you ready for a big challenge? Of course you are! We are going to combine all you've learned so far — the finger patterns, finger placements, rhythmic variations, and slurs and ties. This might take some extra work. Everything you've been doing up to this point has been purposely driving you to be able to play this. If you struggle in a certain section, go back in the book and see which exercise or tune prepares you for that section. Review it a while and then come back.

Practice Pointer: If you section off the piece and practice only the hard spots with a metronome, you'll be light years ahead of where you'd be if you hadn't. Expand slowly, and keep your tempos manageable. Push yourself, but don't go too fast too soon.

A great place to start here is the beginning of the second section. If you begin with the pickup to measure 9, you can instantly apply what you've learned from the high 3 exercises and have great success. Practice this section from the pickup to measure 9 and end on the half note in measure 12. Then practice measure 12 by itself and stop with the first note in measure 13. Then, practice the pickup to measure 13 and end with the first note in measure 14. Continue to overlap as we have here for the rest of the piece. Then try putting these segments together at a slow tempo. Once they are all cohesive, begin increasing the tempo in small increments. You'll be blown away at how fast this will come together – as long as you take your time in the beginning.

28 Picking Up the Pieces

LESSON 8
Double Time...

Don't let the chapter title scare you: It's not time to speed up yet! We're going to practice double up-bows and double down-bows. First, let's see how the double-up motion functions.

In the example that follows, the second two quarter notes have a staccato marking. For the double up-bow here, stop the bow in the middle — before playing the second up-bow. When practicing, there are two ways to consider this situation.

One is to think "down-up-up."

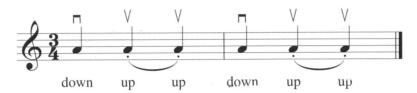

Another is to think "whole-half-half," using your "whole" bow for the down stroke, to get you to the tip. Then, divide the bow in half for the next two up-strokes. Use half the bow for the first up-stroke, and the bottom half for the second consecutive up-stroke.

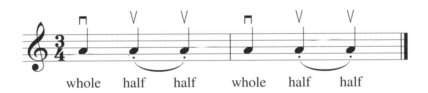

This can be challenging at first, so let's take a simple piece like "Twinkle, Twinkle Little Star" and try the new idea using the fingerings we already know.

29 Double-Up Twinkle

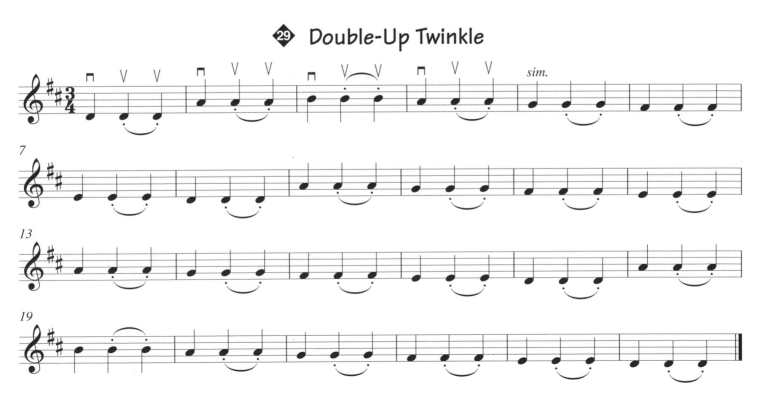

Having accomplished that, we move on to the lifting idea. Lifting is hard to do. It's even harder if you've let your bow grip slip a little. Make sure you spend time double-checking your bow grip. Pinkie is bent and on its tip. Refer back to the pages where we show the bow hold and make sure yours looks right.

Is your bow grip in good order? Great! We are going to practice lifting the bow to do two consecutive down strokes. When you get to the end of the first down stroke, you'll want give a little downward pressure with your pinkie to float the tip off the string. Once you're off the string, in the shape of an arch, and in the air, bring your bow back to the frog. Wait! Before you land back on the string near the frog, think about putting the bow back on the string as if your bow were a commercial jet landing on the tarmac. You want to make sure you place the bow gently before you pull. Be careful not to crash your jet!

When a jet lands, the rear wheels go down first, not the front. Make sure you use your pinkie to set the bow back on the string gracefully. It's tough, so practicing this next piece will help the process.

30 Lifting Twinkle

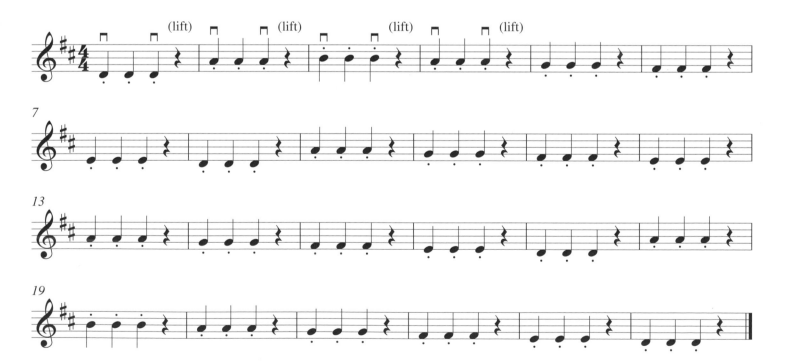

The following exercise uses only down-bows. Give it a try!

🔷31 Down-Down Twinkle

You'll recognize the next tune immediately. It's the famous "Minuet in G" by Christian Petzold, featured in J.S. Bach's *Notebook for Anna Magdalena*.

32 Minuet in G

Everything is getting harder pretty quickly. Work your way through this one and then we'll turn our attention to something a little less demanding. Dig in. This is a tough one!

33 Skip a Rope

LESSON 9

The violin boasts an impressive range of dynamics. That's one of the hardest and best parts about playing the instrument. As violinists, we can play very loud and very soft. The dynamic range is drastic. Performing throughout that dynamic range is an art most of us spend a lifetime improving. Let's explore this concept a bit before you try it.

So far, we've made an effort to keep your sounding point perfectly in between the bridge and fingerboard. We've been working hard at creating confidence in your hands by making a full, loud, clear sound while staying relaxed. Remember, clear and full are always the goal, no matter the dynamic.

A common misconception about sound production is that you have to "push" sound out of the violin. Maybe, in some ways, you do. However, pressure is a result, or better yet, a reaction, to the speed and placement of the bow.

Try this: Compare sounding points with matching bow speeds. To do this, place your bow close to the bridge, maybe a quarter-inch away from it. Put your metronome on 60 beats per minute for four beats per measure. Start at the frog, on the A string, and play the full length of the bow and finish at the end of beat 4 (the fifth click of the metronome). Use gravity to keep the bow on the string and avoid using too much pressure.

Now, play everything exactly the same way, but change your sounding point to a quarter-inch from the fingerboard. What is the difference?

The same amount of bow creates two different volumes, depending on where it is placed. When you play closer to the bridge, you may notice you needed a little more pressure, because there's more resistance there. Thus, pressure is a reaction to bow speed and sounding point.

At the moment, you're doing a lot of reading — and not a lot of playing. Still, it's crucial that you understand what you want from the instrument. Much of what we do on any instrument, particularly a bowed instrument, starts in our minds and translates into our hands. Hang in there for one more explanation.

Here's an outline of musical vocabulary that helps us all know how loud or how soft to play. Much of the music we play uses Italian terms, so you'll learn the Italian name and its English equivalent.

Symbol:	*p*	*mp*	*mf*	*f*
Italian:	piano	mezzo piano	mezzo forte	forte
English:	soft	moderately soft	moderately loud	loud

Using the terms we just learned, we can apply them to something we already know.

◆ 34 Double-Up Twinkle

Now that you have the idea, let's add a little more to it. The dynamics you used above are called *terraced dynamics*. You see a sudden rise or fall in dynamics, rather than a gradual progression either way. To make the transitions smoother and more expressive, we can add crescendos and diminuendos.

Crescendo means to get louder; *diminuendo* means to get quieter. These terms are related to increase and diminish, respectively. A crescendo or diminuendo can either be written out as an abbreviation of the word or with a symbol. These are outlined below.

crescendo   diminuendo

cresc.   *dim.*

Let's see how this fits in a song. Here's a classic.

③⑤ Danny Boy

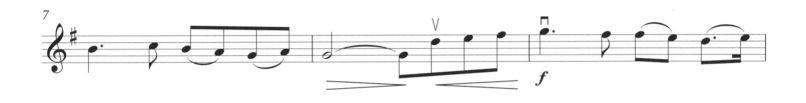

Review, Take 2

Take a few minutes to look over what we've learned so far. It's important that you constantly play what you've already studied to help you continue to improve. This book contains a series of steps designed to propel you forward to your goal of playing well. Let's review.

1. In the beginning, we used the "re-set" idea to help us constantly fix and adjust, to increase our likelihood of success. This can be used to work on the transitions from note to note in any song or piece you play.

2. We then added the first finger pattern.

3. After that, we worked the finger pattern on multiple strings, transitioning gradually and patiently.

4. Then, we complicated it with a rhythm, but used a familiar song to help us keep track of where we were while applying the new techniques.

5. Just when we thought it was getting easy, we added another finger pattern.

6. Then, we worked on that for a little while, still adding a string to keep us moving forward.

7. We used the low 2 idea and went further with it.

8. Next, we stopped and reviewed, much like we're doing now.

9. Then came another finger pattern!

10. We added to our knowledge about counting by studying dotted rhythms and ties.

11. Double up-bows comprised another step. This worked our ability to control bow speed and distribution even more than before. It was tough.

Perhaps the biggest challenge came when we started talking about dynamics. We discussed bow placement vs. bow speed and how they help each other. This might be the hardest part of playing violin. The attention to detail regarding the bow is crucial and difficult, to say the least.

What was the purpose of this review? Well, we're getting close to the end of the book and the last few pieces. It's important to self-assess and figure out what you might be doing wrong, why you're doing it that way, and what you can do to fix it. Take time to go back through all you've learned so far. Play everything! Are the first pieces now easier to pull off than they were when you first started? See if you can improve your quality of sound and consistency with those first exercises.

How to Practice

This part, by far, is where many teachers fall short. Organizing your practice time will make or break your success. Pick up a copy of a practice planner. That's the first step. (I recommend *Musician's Practice Planner*, HL00311358.) Be meticulous about your time management in your practice. Use this breakdown as your base.

Reminder: Your practice sessions should never last more than 45 minutes. If you are going to do a marathon practice, take a 10–15 minute break between sessions. During the break, do not log onto the computer, watch TV, visit Facebook on your smart phone, or do anything else that will distract you and destroy your focus. Get something healthy to eat. Avoid caffeinated drinks and sugary drinks. (Natural sugar from fruits is okay.) Fuel your mind. Finally, stop when you're tired. You've done enough.

Let's get to organizing!

1. Warm Up (10 min)
   - Use the exercises from the beginning of the book as a place to start.
   - Listen to what the violin is doing. Stay relaxed and go slow.
   - Make a quality sound with calculated motions.

2. Technique (10 min)
   - Find an etude or exercise that challenges you.
   - Use exercises that will prepare you for the piece you're working on.
   - Go slow. Take your time. It's important to get your mind wrapped around hard stuff so you can achieve success with the piece.

3. Repertoire (25 min)
   - Repertoire is the piece or pieces you're working on. Practice repertoire in small sections, then expand from there.
   - Go slow. (You've never heard that before, right?)
   - Use the exercises in the book to help you move forward with hard spots.
   - Break it down as small as you need to.
   - Take your time and learn a spot right. It takes less time to learn it right than it does to learn it wrong, and then have to go back and fix it.
   - Always practice with a metronome.
   - Increase your speed only when you've played through your piece with ease at least four consecutive times.
   - Be happy with progress. Perfection is impossible.

4. Cool Down (5 min)
   - Finish up with a piece or song you know well at a good tempo.
   - Before you walk away, make a checklist of things you struggled with. That way, you'll know what to target in your warm-up and technique when you come back to practice again.
   - Set new goals for the next practice.
   - Write down what you did well! Be a positive thinker about your playing.

For those of you who exercise in the gym or at home, you'll notice that this is similar to how a workout operates. That's because it *is* a workout. You may not be curling 50-pound weights, but you're training muscles for endurance and precision. Playing violin takes strength, focus, and determination. All of this is included in any sport.

LESSON 10
Scales...

In Lesson 9, we discussed the importance of reviewing what you've previously learned. We also discussed how to organize your practicing. This can be an addition to your warm-up and/or technique. Remember, in music, it's perfectly acceptable to be an information collector, just as long as you share it, too. When you start working scales into your practice, you can go back and use what you learned before. I still do – and I've been playing for nearly 30 years.

Would you be surprised to discover that you can play several different scales already? It's true! You can! It's all about organizing the finger patterns you've previously learned. Check it out!

36 ◈ G Major Scale – One Octave

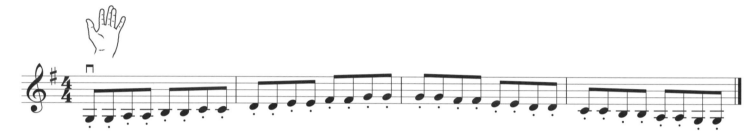

37 ◈ D Major Scale – One Octave

38 ◈ A Major Scale – One Octave

Let's explore the G major scale a bit more. The finger pattern for the last three exercises is exactly the same. You're just starting on a different string each time. If we go to a two-octave G major scale, the finger pattern on the G and D strings is what you've already played. However, when we move to the A and E strings, the finger pattern changes. Now, instead of second and third fingers touching, first and second fingers touch. Let's try it!

39 G Major Scale – Two Octaves

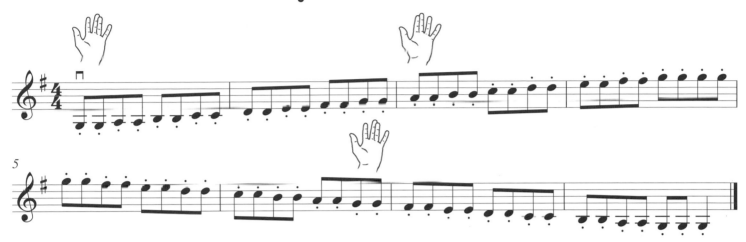

The next scale we will work on is also the same, but different. This time, instead of starting on an open string, we will start with a first finger on G. The note is A and we will play a two-octave A major scale. You already know this finger pattern. The G and D strings will utilize the last finger pattern you learned, where third and fourth finger touch. You could also refer to this as the high 3 pattern. When we get to the A and E strings, though, it's just like the one-octave A major scale exercise you learned on the previous page. Give this one a try!

40 A Major Scale – Two Octaves

LESSON 11
Time to charge admission...

Well, you've made it. The final piece encompasses everything you've learned so far. Remember: Use the exercises in the book to support what you're going to learn next. You're welcome to customize any exercise in this book to fit the piece you're working on. Be creative, be patient, and be positive!

41 Third Time's the Charm